The Midnight Panda

One Sunday night, James wakes up in bed from a nightmare. But is he alone?

James peered at the luminous hands on his clock. It looked odd, as though it was broken – until he realized that both the hands were in a straight line pointing up. It was midnight. The darkest, strangest, scariest part of the night.

He stared out at his room, his eyes fighting with the shadows, trying to work out what all these odd, lumping midnight shapes must be. His bedside table, with a water bottle and a pile of books. The chair in front of his desk. The wardrobe, huge and hulking in the corner. And behind the wardrobe, by the door, growing gradually clearer as his eyes got used to the darkness, was a tall figure. James gulped, his fingers tensing on the edge of his duvet. The figure loomed out from the space between the wardrobe and the door, its fur showing as vague patches of light and dark in the shadows. It was clear, though, what it was.

A bear. Standing in the corner by his wardrobe, and staring at him. A huge bear. In his bedroom.

Was he dreaming again? James screwed his eyes tight shut, hoping that when he opened them again the bear would have disappeared. But it hadn't. It was still there, and it even seemed to be reaching out towards him. Could it see him? Did it know he was there? James peered sideways at the switch for his beside light, as far as he could without moving. It made his eyes hurt, straining them sideways like that, but he didn't care. If he moved, the bear might pounce. Bears were big, but they were fast; he'd watched enough wildlife programmes to know that.

Extract and illustration from *The Midnight Panda* by Holly Webb

Marks

1. Look at the first sentence: *James peered out at the luminous hands on his clock.* Which **two** words below mean the same as the word <u>luminous</u>?

Tick **two**.

flashing ☐

shining ☐

gloomy ☐

glowing ☐

1

2. Why does James think his clock is broken?

_____

_____

_____

2

Marks

3. At what time does James wake up?

_____

_____

1

4. Find and **copy** a phrase or sentence that shows that James is scared.

_____

_____

_____

_____

1

5. Why might James think the bear is a panda?

_____

_____

_____

_____

_____

1

6. What **two** things do you think James is scared of?

1. _____

2. _____

KEEP IT
GOING!

2

Marks

7. *A bear. Standing in the corner by his wardrobe, and staring at him. A huge bear. In his bedroom.*

In this paragraph, the author uses short phrases rather than sentences. What effect does this have?

_____

_____

_____

_____

1

8. Do you think the bear is real?

Tick **one**.

Yes ☐

No ☐

Explain your answer

_____

_____

_____

1

Well done! END OF READING TEST 1!

New Leaf

Today is the first day of my new book.
I've written the date
and underlined it
in red felt-tip
with a ruler.
I'm going to be different
with this book.

With this book
I'm going to be good.
With this book
I'm always going to do the date like that
dead neat
with a ruler
just like Christine Robinson.

With this book
I'll be as clever as Graham Holden,
get all my sums right, be as
neat as Mark Veitch;
I'll keep my pens and pencils
in a pencil case
and never have to borrow again.

With this book
I'm going to work hard,
not talk, be different –
with this book,
not yell out, mess about,
be silly –
with this book.

With this book
I'll be grown-up, sensible,
and everyone will want me;
I'll be picked out first
like Iain Cartwright:
no one will ever laugh at me again.
Everything will be
different

with this book...

By Mick Gowar

Marks

1. Write down **two** examples of why the author might get into trouble in class.

1._____

2._____

_____

2

2. Tick **true** or **false** for each statement about the children in the poem.

Statement	True	False
Christine's work is neat.		
Graham is good at maths.		
Mark has to borrow pens.		
Iain is popular.		

2

3. What do you think the overall theme of this poem is?

Tick **one**.

The writer wants to be cleverer. ☐

The writer wants to have more friends. ☐

The writer wants to change how they are. ☐

The writer wants to do better work. ☐

1

KEEP IT GOING!

Marks

4. The writer repeats the phrase *With this book* many times. Why do you think he does this?

_____

_____

_____

_____

1

5. At the end of the poem, the writer says *Everything will be different.* Do you think everything will be different for him?

Tick **one**.

Yes ☐

No ☐

Explain your answer.

_____

_____

_____

_____

2

6. The poem is called 'New Leaf'. Why do you think the writer has used this title?

_____

_____

_____

2

Well done! END OF READING TEST 2!

Test 3
Reading

Faster than a speeding bullet

The first bullet train left Tokyo station in 1964. It used to take over six and a half hours to travel from the capital of Japan to Osaka. The new train travelled at 130 miles per hour (mph) and cut the journey to four hours. The age of the super-fast *shinkansen* had arrived!

Over fifty years later, Japan's bullet trains have carried more than ten billion people and the *shinkansen* network now covers most of Japan. The trains are also even faster. The speed limit is currently 200mph. It now takes only two and half hours from Tokyo to Osaka. Bullet trains make over one thousand journeys a day. They are almost always on time. The average delay is only 36 seconds!

For passenger comfort, the carriages are sealed like aeroplanes. The ride is smooth as the tracks do not have any joins in them. You won't hear any *clickety-clack*!

The trains are also very safe. Japan is a country affected by volcanic eruptions, tsunamis and typhoons. Despite these dangers, no one has ever been killed in a bullet train crash or derailment. One reason is that the trains have automatic brakes. These detect earthquakes and bring the train to an emergency stop.

Recently, the bullet train has lost its speed crown. For example, a passenger train in China can travel at 216mph. However, the Japanese are working on winning back the title. They will soon introduce a new type of train. These trains don't use wheels. Instead, they use magnets to push or pull the carriages. These maglev trains levitate (float) along the tracks and can travel at over 300mph.

1. How fast do bullet trains now travel in Japan?

Marks

      Tick **one**.

300 miles per hour ☐

130 miles per hour ☐

216 miles per hour ☐

200 miles per hour ☐

1

2. Find and **copy** the names of **two** Japanese cities.

1. _____

2. _____

1

3. What is the Japanese word for <u>bullet train</u>?

_____

_____

1

4. Why don't the train's wheels make a noise?

_____

_____

_____

1

5. Name **two** natural disasters that sometimes affect Japan.

1. _____

2. _____

1

Marks

6. *Recently, the bullet train has lost its speed crown.*

Explain what this sentence means.

_____

_____

_____

1

7. Why are the trains fitted with automatic brakes?

_____

_____

_____

2

8. The word <u>maglev</u> is a combination of two other words. What are those **two** words? Use the final paragraph to help you.

1. _____

2. _____

1

9. What is the main idea of the whole text?

Tick **one**.

Bullet trains used to be fast. ☐

Japan has faster trains than other countries. ☐

Bullet trains have improved people's journeys. ☐

Japan is dangerous but the trains are safe. ☐

1

Well done! END OF READING TEST 3!

14

I Was There... TITANIC

Daisy is sailing to America on board the Titanic. *She meets a boy from first class called Jimmy. And then the ship hits an iceberg.*

The corridors were filling with passengers now: Irish girls with shawls wrapped over their lifebelts, mothers with babies in their arms, and a dozen different languages were all being spoken at the same time. Everywhere was crammed. A steward was guiding women and children up the stairways, but just a few at a time. It was a wide stairway, but not wide enough for everyone trying to get up.

Jimmy and I had spent the whole journey exploring that ship. We knew all the ways around it.

"Stair to the second-class deck," said Jimmy because that was the nearest. "Follow us!"

But when we got to the second-class stair we found another throng of frightened people, all women and children pressing forward. In front of them, two stewards blocked the way.

"They can't do that!" said Jimmy.

"Keep calm!" called one of the stewards. "Stay here, and stay calm!"

But they mustn't stay here, I thought. If the ship really is sinking, they needed to get to the lifeboats. Some were crying, some were praying, some were telling the children that everything would be all right. Above the murmurs of Irish women saying their Hail Marys, I heard something new. It was a creak, then another and another. Something seemed to knock against the side of the ship.

Jimmy and I looked at each other, knowing what that sound meant. On the unsinkable *Titanic* the lifeboats were being lowered, and we were trapped below the decks.

Extract and illustration from *I Was There... TITANIC* by Margi McAllister

Marks

1. Why were some of the people wearing lifebelts?

_____

_____

_____

1

2. Why do the stewards block the stairs?

_____

_____

_____

2

Marks

3. a. What class do you think Daisy and Jimmy are in when the ship hits the iceberg?

Tick one.

First Class ☐

Second Class ☐

Third Class (steerage) ☐

1

b. Explain your answer.

_____

_____

_____

_____

1

4. *Irish women saying their Hail Marys*

What do you think a <u>Hail Mary</u> is?

Tick one.

a type of prayer ☐

a farewell ☐

a greeting ☐

1

KEEP IT GOING!

Marks

5. Daisy hears something knock against the side of the ship. What is it?

_____

_____

1

6. Why are Jimmy and Daisy surprised when they hear the lifeboats being lowered?

_____

_____

_____

1

7. How can you tell from the text that many different types of people were travelling on the *Titanic*?

_____

_____

_____

_____

2

Well done! END OF READING TEST 4!

Keeping the bees busy

Can you still hear buzzing in your garden in the summer? Sadly, your garden is probably quieter than before. That's because the number of bees in the United Kingdom has shrunk. In fact, it has fallen rapidly in the last ten years. Maybe you think that's a good thing. Maybe you're scared of bees. Maybe you find them annoying when you're eating outside. The trouble is, without the bees, we wouldn't have much to eat at all!

There are three types of bee. They all live in different ways. Honeybees live with thousands of other bees in a hive. Solitary bees live alone and sometimes underground. Lastly, bumblebees like living in places such as compost heaps, under sheds or in thick grass.

Bees don't just make delicious honey. When bees visit flowers, they collect nectar to make honey. They also pick up pollen, which they spread to other flowers. This pollen helps plants make fruit, vegetables and seeds. Without the bees spreading the pollen, we would lose about one third of what we eat, including bananas, broccoli and beans.

So where have all the bees gone? First, the bees' habitat is shrinking as towns and cities grow. Warmer weather caused by climate change also affects where the bees can live. Some people say that special chemicals farmers use on crops harm the bees. Lastly, some bee hives are being attacked by viruses.

The good news is that you can help keep those bees buzzing.
Here are some ideas:

- Plant flowers in your garden (bees love purple flowers and ones shaped like tubes).

- Plant a variety of flowers (especially ones that will come out one after the other).

- Keep a compost heap rather than a bin with a lid (bumblebees will burrow to the bottom and set up home).

- Make a bee box from wood blocks and hollow bamboo (this will attract solitary bees).

1. Why might your garden be *quieter than before*?

_____

_____

_____

Marks

1

2. What are the names of the **three** types of bee?

1. _____

2. _____

3. _____

_____

1

3. Some bees are *solitary*. What does <u>solitary</u> mean?

Tick **one**.

They live in hives. ☐   They live alone. ☐

They live underground. ☐   They live in compost heaps. ☐

1

10 MINS

Marks

4. What **two** things do bees take when they visit flowers?

1. _____

2. _____

_____

1

5. Complete the blank sections of the table.

Problem for bees	Caused by
shrinking habitat	
poisoning	
warmer weather	
disease	

2

6. Why would using a compost bin not help bees?

_____

_____

1

Marks

7. More than one of the following sentences are true, but which one best sums up the message of the text as a whole?

Tick one.

Fewer bees means less honey and other food. ☐

We need to look after bees. ☐

Bees face lots of dangers. ☐

Bees are helpful. ☐

1

8. Explain why it is helpful to plant a variety of flowers.

_____

_____

_____

_____

2

Well done! END OF READING TEST 5!

Fight!

Olympic Champion Mo Farah was born in Somalia. He was forced to leave Africa to escape a war. He came to live with his dad in London. This extract from a biography describes his first day at school.

"Say hello to Mohamed, everyone!"

"Hello Mohamed," the class chorused. Out of the corner of his eye, Mo saw that one hard-looking boy had not joined in with the others, but sat, his chair tilted back, with a big sneer on his face.

At break time, some of the other children in the class came up to talk to Mo. He didn't understand what they were saying. He had only learnt three phrases in English: "Excuse me," "Where is the toilet?" and "C'mon then".

The hard-looking boy who had been sneering in class approached Mo. He was still sneering. He muttered something under his breath. It didn't sound very pleasant. Mo decided he had to say something to him. He chose one of the English phrases he'd learnt, though he wasn't sure what it meant.

"C'mon then."

The other boy clenched his fists. "Yeah? Right, you're on!" He gave Mo a shove. Mo shoved him back. Then the boy walloped Mo with his fist.

Mo realised this wasn't like the play fighting he had done at home with his brother. He hit the boy back and soon the two of them were thumping each other hard.

"Fight! Fight!" chorused the boys in the playground.

Two teachers raced out of school. One grabbed Mo and one got hold of the other boy. Then the teachers marched both boys off to the headteacher's office.

When Mo got back to class, he couldn't help but notice the admiring glances from the rest of the children.

Extract and illustration from Dream to Win: Mo Farah by Roy Apps

Marks

1. Where is Somalia?

_____

_____

1

2. What is the name <u>Mo</u> short for?

_____

_____

1

3. *the class chorused*

Which word below means the same as <u>chorused</u>?

Tick **one**.

chanted ☐

shouted ☐

repeated ☐

greeted ☐

1

24

Marks

4. *The hard-looking boy who had been sneering in class approached Mo. He was still sneering. He muttered something under his breath.*

What does this show the boy thinks of Mo?

_____

_____

_____

_____

_____

2

5. Why did the other boy get angry when Mo said, *"C'mon then"*?

_____

_____

_____

1

6. Why did the other children give Mo *admiring glances* after the fight?

_____

_____

1

KEEP IT GOING!

Marks

7. Do you think Mo and the boy will have another fight?

Tick **one**.

Yes ☐

No ☐

Explain your answer.

_____

_____

_____

_____

_____

2

8. In general, what was Mo's first day at school like?

Tick **two**.

boring ☐

confusing ☐

scary ☐

happy ☐

1

Well done! END OF READING TEST 6!

Neon signs in the sky

In northern countries, you may see a mysterious coloured glow in the sky after dark. The glow may be green, blue, orange or red – or even a combination. The strange light seems to float in the air like giant curtains. It sometimes appears as far south as London. This magical light show is the aurora borealis. It is often called the Northern Lights.

An aurora is like a huge neon sign. A neon light bulb contains a special gas that glows when you turn on the electricity. There are gases floating around the Earth too. These gases can be made to glow in a similar way. Of course, nobody is pushing a switch to make the sky glow. The gases glow when they are hit by charged particles that come all the way from the Sun.

Particles shoot out from the Sun every day. However, sometimes there are great electrical storms on the Sun. These storms fling out huge bursts of particles towards the Earth. These particles travel at a million miles per hour until they hit the Earth's magnetic field, which is an invisible shield around our planet. The magnetic field deflects some of the particles towards the North Pole. This makes the air glow and the incredible light show begins. Particles are also pushed towards the South Pole. This causes a similar aurora called the aurora australis.

However, these pretty lights can be dangerous. They affect satellites, aeroplanes and even crews in spacecraft. To help protect us, scientists watch "the weather" on the Sun and warn us when there might be powerful solar storms in the next few days.

Marks

1. In the first paragraph, the writer uses a simile to describe the aurora.

a. What is the aurora described as being like?

_____

1

b. Why does the writer use a simile like this to describe the aurora?

_____

_____

_____

1

2. *An aurora is like a huge neon sign.* What do you think <u>neon</u> is?

_____

_____

1

3. What causes the gases in the sky to glow?

Tick **one.**

the Sun ☐

electricity ☐

the magnetic field ☐

charged particles ☐

1

Marks

4. Fill in the **two** blank sections in this table.

Name	Alternative name
aurora borealis	
	Southern Lights

2

5. Find and **copy one** word from the final paragraph that means <u>from the Sun</u>.

_____

1

6. Number these events (1–4) to show the order in which they happen.

The sky seems to glow with coloured lights.	
Scientists warn people about storm activity on the Sun.	
The particles hit the Earth's magnetic field and are pushed towards the poles.	
Charged particles shoot out from the Sun.	

1

7. Why can you only see an aurora in the north or the south?

_____

_____

_____

2

Well done! END OF READING TEST 7!

Test 8
Reading

Anne and the Fieldmouse

We found a mouse in the chalk quarry today
In a circle of stones and empty oil drums
By the fag end of a fire. There had been
A picnic there: he must have been after the crumbs.

Jane saw him first, a flicker of brown fur
In and out of the charred wood and chalk-white.
I saw him last, but not till we'd turned up
Every stone and surprised him into flight,

Though not far – little zigzag spurts from stone
To stone. Once, as he lurked in his hiding-place,
I saw his beady eyes uplifted to mine.
I'd never seen such terror in so small a face.

I watched, amazed and guilty. Beside us suddenly
A heavy pheasant whirred up from the ground,
Scaring us all; and, before we knew it, the mouse
Had broken cover, skimming away without a sound,

Melting into the nettles. We didn't go
Till I'd chalked in capitals on a rusty can:
THERE'S A MOUSE IN THOSE NETTLES. LEAVE
HIM ALONE. NOVEMBER 15th. ANNE.

By Ian Serraillier

Marks

1. Name **two** non-living objects that were in the quarry.

1. _____

2. _____

_____

◯

1

2. Why do you think the mouse was near the fire? Explain using evidence from the text.

_____

_____

_____

_____

◯

2

3. The wood is *charred*. What does <u>charred</u> mean?

Tick **one**.

on fire ☐

burned ☐

turned to ash ☐

hot ☐

◯

1

4. Explain why Jane was able to see the mouse.

_____

_____

_____

◯

2

Marks

5. Apart from the mouse, what other animal did they see?

_____

_____

○ 1

6. *I watched, amazed and guilty.*

Why did the narrator feel <u>guilty</u>?

_____

_____

_____

○ 1

7. Where does the mouse end up hiding?

Tick one.

under a stone ☐

in the fireplace ☐

under a rusty can ☐

in some nettles ☐

○ 1

8. What did the narrator of the poem do just before she left the quarry?

_____

_____

○ 1

Well done! END OF READING TEST 8!

33

My Vesak celebration

May lives in Bristol, but her family came from Thailand. They are Buddhists. Once a year, they celebrate May's favourite festival, called Vesak. May explains why she enjoys Vesak so much.

I can't wait for the full moon! My friends think I'm strange. They say a full moon means that spooky witches and werewolves come out. But for me, it means Vesak has arrived!

Vesak is our most important festival. It takes place when there's a full moon in the month of May. We think about the man who started our religion, Buddha. Vesak is special because it is Buddha's birthday. It is also the day that Buddha found enlightenment. This means he worked out the meaning of life.

In the morning, I start by opening my Happy Vesak Day cards from my family. Then we go to the temple. We offer food, candles and flowers to the statues at the altar. The monk bathes a small statue of Buddha with scented water. This reminds us to wash away bad things like greed and hatred. I love the chanting and the prayers, but I'm still learning how to meditate properly. I find it boring because I keep thinking about my favourite activity: making paper lanterns. I work with my family to make a big one out of tissue paper and bamboo. It helps us practise what the monks teach us: we have to work together and treat each other with respect.

Later, we have a special meal. The food is always vegetarian as we don't eat meat on Vesak. It's okay but I wish we had chicken satay! We often have a procession too, where we display our lanterns and Buddhist flags.

There's one more reason I love Vesak: it always takes place in May!

1. What religion is May?

_____

2. What might you see in the sky on Vesak?

_____

Marks

1

1

KEEP IT GOING!

Marks

3. *It is also the day that Buddha found enlightenment.*

Which word most closely matches the meaning of the word
<u>enlightenment</u>?

Tick **one**.

brightness ☐

excitement ☐

wisdom ☐

information ☐

1

4. Find and **copy one** thing May gives and **one** thing she receives
on Vesak.

Gives: _____

Receives: _____

2

5. One of May's friends thinks all Buddhists are vegetarians.
Are they correct?

Tick **one**.

Yes ☐

No ☐

Explain why.

_____

_____

_____

1

Marks

6. Number these Vesak activities in the order that you think May enjoys them (with number 1 being the most enjoyable).

Eating a special meal	
Making paper lanterns	
Chanting and praying	
Meditation	

1

7. *There's one more reason I love Vesak: it always takes place in May!*

Why do you think the author writes this?

_____

_____

1

8. How does celebrating Vesak help Buddhists to become better people? Give evidence from the text to explain your answer.

_____

_____

_____

_____

_____

_____

2

Well done! END OF READING TEST 9!

The Big Wish

Sam isn't just granted one wish; he is given a million. He's always wanted to be an invincible superhero. But every superhero needs an arch-enemy, right? In this extract, they fight in the sky above Sam's house.

I steadied myself, thrust my fists out in front of me and power-dived at him at top-speed. He didn't try to get out of my way but flew straight towards me.

We met with a terrific clatter in the middle of the sky and bounced apart. But he recovered first. I was still spinning in the air when I felt his drill bite into my chest. At the same time the circular saw started to chew into my neck, and the hammer-hand was whacking me on the back of the head.

This was…too much. 'I wish you couldn't fly any more, Power-Tool Man,' I shouted, and immediately he plunged away from me and spiralled towards the earth. He hit the ground with a crash that was loud even from a hundred metres up.

He wasn't hurt though, what with being super strong. He bounced straight back up on to his feet. I zoomed down towards him. He started winding his hammer-hand up, whirling it round to get ready for a mighty blow. But I wasn't having it. 'I wish you were as weak as a kitten!' I said. So he stood there, all helpless and tottering, not strong enough even to raise his power-tool arms. I landed beside him and gave him a little push in his workbench-chest and he fell on his back.

'Do you surrender, Power-Tool Man?'

'No, I'll never surrender!'

'I wish you would.'

'Oh, all right, I surrender, then.'

'Another awesome victory for Awesome Man!' I said. But it didn't feel all that awesome. I was fed up. 'I wish you didn't exist any more, Power-Tool Man.'

'I don't.'

And he was gone.

Extract from *The Big Wish* by Brandon Robshaw

Marks

1. *But every superhero needs an arch-enemy, right?*

What is an <u>arch-enemy</u>?

_____

_____

1

2. Power-Tool Man is armed with **three** tools. What are they?

1. _____

2. _____

3. _____

1

3. Tick **true** or **false** for each statement about Sam's wishes.

Statement	True	False
Power-Tool Man falls down because Sam wishes he would fall asleep.		
Power-Tool Man gives up because Sam wishes he would surrender.		
Power-Tool Man is helpless because Sam wishes he was weak.		
Power-Tool Man disappears because Sam wishes there were no more villains.		

2

KEEP IT GOING!

Marks

4. Look at the paragraph beginning *He wasn't hurt though, what with being super strong.*

Find and **copy one** word that means <u>unstable</u>.

_____

_____

1

5. Why did Sam feel *fed up* at the end?

_____

_____

_____

_____

_____

2

6. What is Sam's superhero name?

_____

_____

1

7. Sam has a million wishes. Thinking about this extract, what do you think he will do with them?

_____

_____

_____

_____

2

Well done! END OF READING TEST 10!

Answers
Reading

Q	Mark scheme for Reading Test 1: The Midnight Panda	Marks
1	**Award 1 mark** for both correct: shining, glowing	1
2	**Award 2 marks** for an answer that refers to one of the clock hands being hidden by the other, such as: Both the hands were pointing straight up, meaning it looked like one of them was missing. **Award 1 mark** for an answer referring to both clock hands pointing straight up but without explaining the effect.	1
3	**Award 1 mark** for: midnight OR 12 o'clock at night	2
4	**Award 1 mark** for one of the following: *his eyes fighting with the shadows* OR *James gulped, his fingers tensing on the edge of his duvet.* OR *James screwed his eyes tight shut, hoping that when he opened them again the bear would have disappeared.* OR *James peered sideways at the switch for his beside light, as far as he could without moving.*	1
5	**Award 1 mark** for an answer that refers to the nature of the fur, such as: The bear's fur had patches of light and dark, like a panda's.	1
6	**Award 1 mark** for each correct answer: 1. bears 2. the dark/night	2
7	**Award 1 mark** for an answer that refers to how the text is made more dramatic, such as: It makes it seem scarier. OR It makes it more shocking, surprising and tense.	1
8	**Award 1 mark** for either Yes or No with an appropriate explanation based on the evidence, such as: No, because James is just seeing things because he's scared of the dark. Yes, because the author describes the bear's fur.	1
	Total	10

Q	Mark scheme for Reading Test 2: New Leaf	Marks
1	**Award 2 marks** for any two of the following: not working hard; talking; yelling out; messing about; being silly **Award 1 mark** for any one of the above.	2
2	**Award 2 marks** for all four answers correct. **Award 1 mark** for two or three correct answers. | Statement	True	False | |---|---|---| | Christine's work is neat. | ✔ | | | Graham is good at maths. | ✔ | | | Mark has to borrow pens. | | ✔ | | Iain is popular. | ✔ | |	2
3	**Award 1 mark** for: The writer wants to change how they are.	1
4	**Award 1 mark** for an answer that refers to the writer's determination, such as: It shows that the writer really wants to do better as it's like he's making a promise to his book.	1
5	**Award 2 marks** for an answer that fully justifies either choice with reasons from the poem, such as: Yes, because he really wants to do better and stop being silly, even though it might be hard. No, because he does too many things wrong and I don't think he can change all of them because it's just who he is. **Award 1 mark** for an answer that justifies either choice with simpler reasons, such as: Yes, because he doesn't want to borrow pens anymore. No, because he talks too much.	2

Q	Mark scheme for Reading Test 2: New Leaf	Marks
6	**Award 2 marks** for an answer that refers to making a fresh start and link to the expression 'turning over a new leaf.' For example: If you turn over a new leaf, it means you want to make a change, like the author does. **Award 1 mark** for an answer that refers to making a fresh start but not the idiom, such as: The author wants to be a new person, like a new leaf.	2
	Total	10

Q	Mark scheme for Reading Test 3: Faster than a speeding bullet	Marks
1	**Award 1 mark** for: 200 miles per hour	1
2	**Award 1 mark** for both correct: 1. Tokyo 2. Osaka	1
3	**Award 1 mark** for: shinkansen	1
4	**Award 1 mark** for an answer that refers to the tracks not having any joins in them.	1
5	**Award 1 mark** for any two of: volcanic eruptions, tsunamis, typhoons, earthquakes	1
6	**Award 1 mark** for an answer that shows an understanding that the bullet train was once the fastest but this is no longer true, such as: It was once the fastest but now there are trains in China that go faster.	1
7	**Award 2 marks** for an answer that refers to preventing derailment during an earthquake, such as: The brakes stop the train in an earthquake so the train doesn't come off the tracks. **Award 1 mark** for an answer that refers to stopping in an earthquake but not derailment.	2
8	**Award 1 mark** for: magnetic/magnet and levitation/levitate (Do not allow float.)	1
9	**Award 1 mark** for: Bullet trains have improved people's journeys.	1
	Total	10

Q	Mark scheme for Reading Test 4: I was there... *Titanic*	Marks
1	**Award 1 mark** for an answer that refers to the ship sinking, such as: They thought the ship might be sinking.	1
2	**Award 2 marks** for an answer that recognises that they are trying to control the crowd and keep people safe, such as: Because there is not enough room for everyone to get up the stairs all at once and people may get crushed. **Award 1 mark** where only one of these reasons is given.	2
3	**a. Award 1 mark** for: third class (steerage) **b. Award 1 mark** for an answer that refers to how Daisy and Jimmy are trying to go up the second-class stairs, such as: Daisy and Jimmy are stuck and can't get up to the second-class deck.	2
4	**Award 1 mark** for: a type of prayer	1
5	**Award 1 mark** for: a lifeboat (being lowered)	1
6	**Award 1 mark** for an answer that refers to the *Titanic* supposedly being unsinkable.	1
7	**Award 2 marks** for an answer that refers to the number of languages spoken and that there were rich as well as poor people, such as: People were from all around the word because they were speaking a dozen different languages and there were rich people in first class and poor people in third class. **Award 1 mark** where only one of these reasons is given.	2
	Total	10

Q	Mark scheme for Reading Test 5: Keeping the bees busy	Marks
1	**Award 1 mark** for an answer that refers to a fall in numbers of bees, such as: The number of bees has gone down. Do not accept answers that suggest that there are no bees left.	1
2	**Award 1 mark** for all three answers correct: 1. honeybee 2. solitary bee 3. bumblebee	1
3	**Award 1 mark** for: They live alone.	1
4	**Award 1 mark** for both correct: 1. nectar (not honey) 2. pollen	1
5	**Award 2 marks** for all four of the following correct. **Award 1 mark** for three correct. <table><tr><td>**Problem for bees**</td><td>**Caused by**</td></tr><tr><td>shrinking habitat</td><td>(growing) towns and cities</td></tr><tr><td>poisoning</td><td>special chemicals (used by farmers on crops)</td></tr><tr><td>warmer weather</td><td>climate change</td></tr><tr><td>disease</td><td>viruses</td></tr></table>	2
6	**Award 1 mark** for an answer that refers to the lid blocking the bees, such as: The lid would stop the bees from getting in.	1
7	**Award 1 mark** for: We need to look after bees.	1
8	**Award 2 marks** for an answer that refers to how flowers that bloom over time provide food for the bees for longer, such as: Flowers that come out one after the other mean the bees don't have all their food at the same time. **Award 1 mark** for an answer that only refers to how different flowers bloom at different times, but without the link to food.	2
	Total	10

Q	Mark scheme for Reading Test 6: Fight!	Marks
1	**Award 1 mark** for: Africa	1
2	**Award 1 mark** for: Mohamed	1
3	**Award 1 mark** for: chanted	1
4	**Award 2 marks** for an answer that refers to how the boy's sneering and muttering indicate that he doesn't like Mo, such as: It shows the boy doesn't like Mo, because he's looking at him in a horrible way and probably saying rude things under his breath. **Award 1 mark** for an answer that refers to how the boy doesn't like Mo but doesn't expand on how his sneering and muttering show this.	2
5	**Award 1 mark** for an answer that suggests he thought Mo wanted a fight/was inviting him to fight.	1
6	**Award 1 mark** for an answer such as: They were impressed because Mo had fought the mean boy.	1
7	**Award 2 marks** for an answer that fully justifies either choice and refers directly to the boys' behaviour, such as: Yes, because the other boy really seems to dislike Mo and may want to fight with him again. No, because Mo defended himself and the other boy will probably not want to get into a fight with him again. **Award 1 mark** for an answer that justifies either choice with simpler, more general reasons, such as: Yes, because they won't be friends. No, because the teachers will tell them off.	2
8	**Award 1 mark** for both correct: confusing, scary	1
	Total	10

Q	Mark scheme for Reading Test 7: Neon signs in the sky	Marks
1	a. **Award 1 mark** for: giant curtains b. **Award 1 mark** for an answer that explains that the simile helps the reader to visualise the aurora, such as: It makes it easier for the reader to imagine the lights if they haven't seen them before.	2
2	**Award 1 mark** for: a gas	1
3	**Award 1 mark** for: charged particles	1
4	**Award 1 mark** for each correct answer:	2

Name	Alternative name
aurora borealis	**Northern Lights**
aurora australis	Southern Lights

Q		Marks
5	**Award 1 mark** for: solar	1
6	**Award 1 mark** for the correct order: (4) The sky seems to glow with coloured lights. (1) Scientists warn people about storm activity on the Sun. (3) The particles hit the Earth's magnetic field and are pushed towards the poles. (2) Charged particles shoot out from the Sun.	1
7	**Award 2 marks** for an answer that refers to how the magnetic field deflects the particles to the north and south, meaning the aurora only takes place there. For example: The Earth's magnetic field pushes the particles towards the North Pole and the South Pole, so auroras don't happen anywhere else. **Award 1 mark** for an answer that refers to how the magnetic field deflects the particles.	2
	Total	10

Q	Mark scheme for Reading Test 8: Anne and the Fieldmouse	Marks
1	**Award 1 mark** for any two of: chalk, stones, oil drums, fire, crumbs, rusty can	1
2	**Award 2 marks** for an answer that includes appropriate evidence from the text to support it, such as: The mouse wanted to eat the crumbs from the picnic because it says *he must've been after the crumbs.* **Award 1 mark** for an answer which refers to the mouse wanting to eat the crumbs but without quoting directly from the text.	2
3	**Award 1 mark** for: burned	1
4	**Award 2 marks** for an answer that refers to the fact that the mouse was moving, and the contrast between the colour of the mouse and the colour of its surroundings, such as: The mouse was moving and its brown fur stood out from the burned wood and the white chalk. **Award 1 mark** for an answer that refers to how Jane saw it moving.	2
5	**Award 1 mark** for: a pheasant	1
6	**Award 1 mark** for an answer such as: The mouse looked so scared. OR They scared the mouse trying to find it.	1
7	**Award 1 mark** for: in some nettles	1
8	**Award 1 mark** for an answer that refers to the message as a warning, such as: She wrote a warning on a rusty can. OR She wrote a message to warn people not to disturb the mouse.	1
	Total	10

Q	Mark scheme for Reading Test 9: My Vesak celebration	Marks
1	**Award 1 mark** for: Buddhist	1
2	**Award 1 mark** for: a full moon	1
3	**Award 1 mark** for: wisdom	1
4	**Award 1 mark** each for: Gives: food, candles or flowers (any one of these) Receives: a Happy Vesak Day card	2
5	**Award 1 mark** for: No, and answers that refer to Buddhists being required to be vegetarian on Vesak only, such as: Buddhists can't eat meat on Vesak but can on other days.	1
6	**Award 1 mark** for the correct order: (3) Eating a special meal (1) Making paper lanterns (2) Chanting and praying (4) Meditation	1
7	**Award 1 mark** for an answer that refers to the link between her name and the month, such as: Her name is also May.	1
8	**Award 2 marks** for an answer that includes an example, with evidence, such as: Vesak helps Buddhists to become better people because when they see the Buddha statue being washed it reminds them to wash away their own bad things like greed and hatred. OR When Buddhists make a lantern with their whole family, they have to work together and treat each other with respect. **Award 1 mark** for an answer that gives an example without an explanation, such as: Vesak reminds Buddhists to wash away bad things like greed and hatred. OR Vesak helps Buddhists to work together.	2
	Total	10

Q	Mark scheme for Reading Test 10: The Big Wish	Marks
1	**Award 1 mark** for an answer that refers to a main or principal adversary, such as: his worst enemy	1
2	**Award 1 mark** (if all three correct) for: 1. drill, 2. (circular) saw 3. hammer	1
3	**Award 2 marks** for all four correct. **Award 1 mark** for two or three correct answers. _(see table below)_	2

Statement	True	False
Power-Tool Man falls down because Sam wishes he would fall asleep.		✔
Power-Tool Man gives up because Sam wishes he would surrender.	✔	
Power-Tool Man is helpless because Sam wishes he was weak.	✔	
Power-Tool Man disappears because Sam wishes there were no more villains.		✔

Q		Marks
4	**Award 1 mark** for: tottering	1
5	**Award 2 marks** for an answer that refers to Sam feeling that his victory was too easy because he used his wishes, such as: Sam was fed up because he didn't really feel like he had beaten his enemy because he just wished it to happen and it was too easy. **Award 1 mark** for an answer that refers to Sam feeling that his victory was too easy, but not the reason.	2
6	**Award 1 mark** for: Awesome Man	1
7	**Award 2 marks** for an answer that predicts how Sam may use his wishes based on his dissatisfaction with them and that includes a reasoned explanation. For example: I think Sam will wish away his wishes because he seems fed up with them already as it was too easy for him to beat his enemy. **Award 1 mark** for an answer that makes a prediction about a positive or negative wish, but without direct reference to Sam's state of mind. For example: I think he will make lots of wishes to help people instead of fighting.	2
	Total	10

Question type 1

Explain the meaning of words

What to expect

Some questions ask you to think about the meaning of certain words. The word is likely to be unfamiliar or it may have more than one meaning. You will need to look at the word in context. This means you will have to consider the words that come before and after to help you understand the word's meaning. Don't just guess. The context will provide the clues.

Example

Alexa was really excited. Her favourite author had just posted some amazing news on social media. After a three-year wait, there was going to be a brand new *Barry Spotter* novel in the autumn. But when Alexa read more about it, she frowned: there would be no book to buy. Instead, the author was taking the novel approach of publishing the story chapter-by-chapter on a website. Alexa thought that sounded weird.

1. Look at the paragraph beginning *Alexa was really excited...*

Which word most closely matches the meaning of the word <u>unusual</u>?

      Tick **one**.

amazing ☐

novel ☑

social ☐

weird ☐

1 mark

Explanation: Although *weird* can mean *unusual,* the word that most closely matches the meaning of *unusual* is *novel.* The word *novel* occurs twice in the paragraph: as a noun meaning a story book; and as an adjective meaning unusual. The context provides the clues: Alexa's reaction is to frown because *there would be no book to buy,* which sounds *weird* to her, suggesting there is something unusual about how the story is going to be published (*chapter-by-chapter on a website*).

Question type 2
Find and record information

What to expect

Some questions ask you to find a particular piece of information or identify key details in a piece of fiction or non-fiction. You will need to scan the text to quickly find a word or phrase. You will often be expected to copy out the information word for word from the text.

Example

Brushing your teeth regularly is very important. Firstly, it helps prevent tooth decay. Even though your teeth are very hard on the outside, they can become damaged, which leads to painful toothache. Another reason to brush your teeth twice a day is to prevent gum disease. Gingivitis is a painful inflammation of the gums where they meet your teeth. Both tooth decay and gum disease are caused by plaque, which is a build-up of food and bacteria in the mouth.

1. What are the two main reasons to brush your teeth? **Find** and **copy two** phrases from the text.

1. _it helps prevent tooth decay_

2. _it helps prevent gum disease_

I mark

Explanation: The two main reasons are given at separate points within the paragraph. The key to answering this question is to recognise that the word *prevent* introduces both reasons. The rest of the information in the paragraph explains more about the two reasons given and shouldn't be used to answer the question. For example, *painful toothache* would not be acceptable as the copied phrase does not mention how brushing *prevents* it.

Question type 3
Summarise the main ideas

What to expect

Some questions ask you to identify the main point or message from a number of paragraphs or the text as a whole. You will not need to write a summary yourself, but choose from some likely options. You may need to skim read the text again to get an overall grasp of how to answer the question.

Example

What you eat affects how you feel today, but will also affect your future. Good nutrition is essential to leading a healthy lifestyle. Along with regular exercise, a healthy diet can keep you well today and reduce the risk of dangerous diseases as you get older. There are lots of ways to eat healthily: eat lots of fresh fruit and veg; try whole-grain cereals; switch to low-fat milk; choose lean protein; cut back on fatty, processed food; and drink water instead of sugary drinks. It's easier than you think if you take small steps each week to improve your nutrition today and to protect you from problems in the years to come.

1. Thinking about the text as a whole, what is the main message?

Tick **one.**

Fatty foods should be cut back as part of a healthy diet. ☐

Regular exercise is an important part of leading a healthy lifestyle. ☐

Dangerous diseases are caused by a poor diet. ☐

Improving your diet will make you healthier now and in the future. ✔

1 mark

Explanation: All four of the choices contain correct information. However, only the final option summarises a point which is made a number of times in the paragraph (your diet affects your health now and in the future). The other options concentrate too narrowly on more specific ideas and not this main message.

Skills check

Question type 4
Make inferences

What to expect

Some questions ask you to 'read between the lines'. In other words, the meaning of a piece of writing may not be completely obvious. Sometimes you will need to work out what the writer means from clues in the text. This is called making an inference. You may also be asked to justify your reasons for making the inference by using evidence from the text.

Example

Caleb and his brother Freddie were in New York. In Midtown Manhattan, the Empire State Building towered over them. Caleb smiled. It was taller and more magnificent that he had imagined. He turned to his brother. "Well, what are we waiting for?" he asked. "There's no queue. We can take a lift straight to the top."

Freddie glanced up at the skyscraper. It seemed to go on up and up forever. He gulped and felt his legs shake unsteadily beneath him. "I think we should go to Central Park first," he replied. "It will be dark soon otherwise. We can come back here another day."

1. What evidence is there that Freddie doesn't like heights?

He doesn't like heights because he seems scared. He swallows nervously and feels a bit shaky. He also makes an excuse that they should go to a different place because he is trying to put off going to the top of the building.

2 marks

Explanation: The writer never says that *Freddie was scared of heights*. However, the clues are there in the text. Reading between the lines, you can make the inference that his nervous behaviour and his excuse indicate that he does not like heights. To achieve both marks, you would need to mention both his nervousness and his excuse as evidence.

Question type 5

Make predictions

What to expect

Some questions ask you to explain what you think will happen next. This is called making a prediction. Like making an inference, you should always make your prediction based on evidence from the text. Don't guess. Use what's happened already to make a reasoned decision about what happens next.

Example

Ella raised her hands confidently to the piano keyboard. This was her moment. Her chance to shine. As always, she had practised for hour after hour. She knew the piece inside out: her fingers would take over and skittle up and down the black and white keys almost with a mind of their own. Ella allowed herself a glance at the audience. It was a mistake. She caught a glimpse of her mum, who gave her a tense smile. Over her mother's shoulder, Ella spotted the long table at which sat the three stony-faced, silent judges. The butterflies took flight in Ella's stomach. She glanced back down at her hands and noticed that her fingers were trembling slightly.

1. What does this paragraph suggest might happen next?

It suggests that Ella will not perform her piano piece well because she made the mistake of looking at the judges and losing her confidence.

2 marks

Explanation: Making a prediction often involves making inferences too. Here you can infer that Ella's nerves are triggered by seeing the judges. The writer calls this a mistake. You can infer from this that things are not going to go as planned in the performance. To achieve both marks, you would need to mention how her mistake (looking at the judges) might affect her performance.

Question type 6

Show how language, structure and presentation add to meaning

What to expect

Some questions ask you to identify how the author's choice of language, structure and presentation make the meaning of the whole text clear. You might need to show how a story is structured or find key moments that affect the overall meaning. You might be asked how particular words or phrases make the meaning clearer.

Example

Roxanne wiped a bead of sweat from the corner of her eye. The sun was beating down steadily. As Roxanne crossed the park, the still summer air stirred lazily. For a moment, a soothing breeze brushed gently across her hot face. The leaves in the trees fluttered briefly but came to rest again. It reminded Roxanne of a sleepy cat stretching for a moment before returning to its peaceful slumber.

1. **Find** and **copy four** words or phrases from the paragraph that suggest a calm scene.

1. _still_

2. _soothing_

3. _sleepy_

4. _peaceful_

2 marks

Explanation: Any four of: still, stirred lazily, soothing (breeze), (brushed) gently, fluttering briefly, came to rest, sleepy, peaceful (slumber) would be acceptable. All of the words and phrases listed are used by the author to 'paint a picture' of a hot, peaceful summer's day in a park where a breeze briefly disturbs the calm scene.

Question type 7

Explain how certain words and phrases enhance meaning

What to expect

Some questions ask you to look closely at the author's choice of language. You might be asked how particular words or phrases create atmosphere, or make an image more vivid or easier to imagine. These questions can be quite similar to question type 6, but you will be asked to give your own impressions and to interpret the text more deeply.

Example

> Roxanne wiped a bead of sweat from the corner of her eye. The sun was beating down steadily. As Roxanne crossed the park, the still summer air stirred lazily. For a moment, a soothing breeze brushed gently across her hot face. The leaves in the trees fluttered briefly but came to rest again. It reminded Roxanne of a sleepy cat stretching for a moment before returning to its peaceful slumber.

1. What does the following phrase tell you about the kind of day it is in the story?
   a sleepy cat stretching for a moment before returning to its peaceful slumber

It shows what a hot, restful kind of day it is: like a lazy cat that can't be bothered to move, apart from to stretch, even the leaves on the trees can hardly move.

2 marks

Explanation: This simile is used by the author to 'paint a picture' of a hot, peaceful summer's day in a park where a short breeze is the only movement. To be awarded both marks, you would be expected to identify the effect of the language, and give an explanation as to why you think this.

Progress chart

Fill in your score in the table below
to see how well you've done.

	Score
Test 1	
Test 2	
Test 3	
Test 4	
Test 5	
Test 6	
Test 7	
Test 8	
Test 9	
Test 10	
TOTAL	

Mark	
0–34	Good try! You need more practice in some topics – ask an adult to help you.
35–69	You're doing really well. Ask for extra help for any topics you found tricky.
70–100	You're a 10-Minute SATs Test reading star – good work!

GREAT WORK!

Reward Certificate

Well done!

*You have completed all of the
10-Minute SATs Tests*

Name: _____ Date: _____

SCHOLASTIC

Prepare for SATs Success

Find out more at www.scholastic.co.uk/assessment

QUICK TESTS FOR SATs SUCCESS

BOOST YOUR CHILD'S CONFIDENCE WITH 10-MINUTE SATs TESTS

- Bite-size mini SATs tests which take just 10 minutes to complete
- Covers key National Test topics
- Full answers and progress chart provided to track improvement
- Available for Years 1 to 6

Find out more at www.scholastic.co.uk

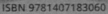

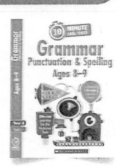